LET'S GET
DRESSED

WRITTEN & ILLUSTRATED BY
RUTH WALTON

SEA-TO-SEA

Mankato Collingwood London

Every day, when we wake
up in the morning,
we put on our clothes.

What do you put on first?

Can you see it here?

Underneath our other clothes, we wear underwear.

Most underwear is made of **cotton**, because it's nice and soft.

Do you know what cotton is?

Cotton is a **natural fiber** that comes from cotton plants. They grow in many countries, including India, China, and the United States. Cotton is a thirsty plant and needs a lot of water while it's growing!

cotton flower

Cotton Creepy-Crawlies!

All of these insects love living on cotton plants...

To kill the insect pests, farmers often use **pesticides,** *which can harm the environment.*

Organic *cotton is grown using natural pest controls.*

Boll weevil

Thrip

Army-worm

After the plant has flowered, its petals drop off and the seed pods grow. They are called cotton **bolls**.

cotton boll

It takes about 7 to 10 weeks for the cotton bolls to grow fully.

Then the bolls pop open and they are ready to be harvested.

The cotton is harvested, and taken to a factory to be **processed**.

In the factory, the cotton is washed and spun into **thread**.

The thread can be **woven** on a **loom**, or **knitted** on a machine to become **fabric**.

This fabric is woven...

...and this fabric is knitted.

8

The fabric can be **dyed** or colorful inks can be printed onto it.

At a different factory, the fabric is made into clothes, using sewing machines.

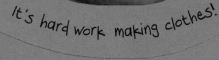
It's hard work making clothes!

All of these clothes are made of cotton...

T-shirt

Skirt

Underpants

Socks

Jeans

Shirt

Are you wearing any cotton clothing?

9

Most clothes have **fasteners** on them to stop them from falling off! **Zippers** and **buttons** are common types of fastener.

Do you know how a zipper works?

These are the teeth.

Zippers have two small rows of teeth, which lock together when the slider glides over them, and unlock on the way back.

This is the "slider."

When Were Zippers Invented?

Zippers were first invented in 1851. Over the next 60 years, several people improved the design. Finally, in the 1920s and 1930s, zippers were at last used on many clothes.

The History of Buttons...
Buttons were invented around 3,000 years ago, but were only used as decoration. By the thirteenth century buttons were being used as fasteners. Before then, people often tied their clothes on with laces, the same way we use laces on our shoes!

Are there any fasteners on the clothes you are wearing today?

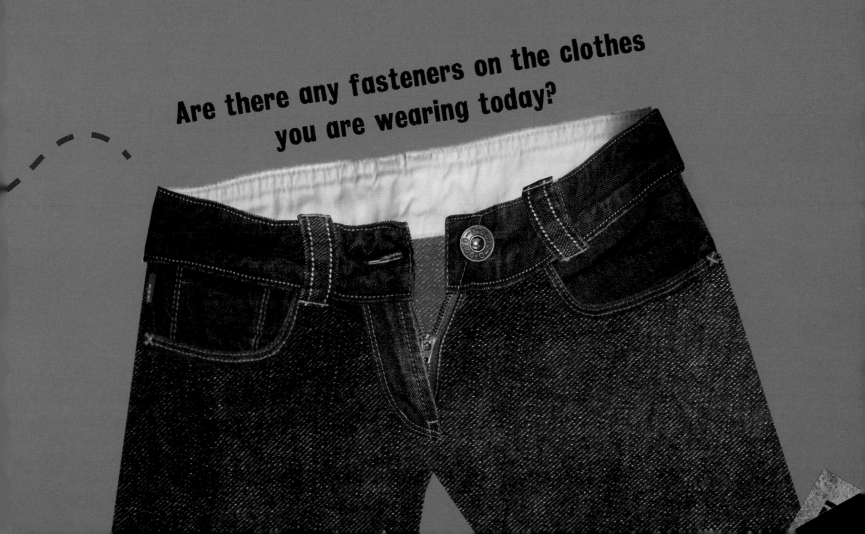

When it's cold outside, we wear warm clothes.

What can you think of that is warm to wear?

What is it made out of?

Wool is a natural fiber that is very cozy
and good at keeping us snug in cold weather.

Which animal does wool come from?

Goat

Camel

Alpaca

Rabbit

Wool can come from all of these animals!
But most wool we wear comes from **sheep**.

In winter, sheep grow long coats called **fleeces**, to keep themselves warm.

In the spring, farmers cut the fleeces off the sheep. This is called **shearing**.

The farmer shears the sheep using electric clippers.

He has to hold the sheep tightly so it doesn't escape!

The wool is washed to make sure it's nice and clean.

Here is a farmer shearing his sheep!

Wool can be dyed many colors.

When the wool is dry, it is combed to untangle the fibers, just like combing your hair!

Then the wool is spun into **yarn**, and made into clothes.

16

Most wool clothing is knitted on a machine.

Knitting can also be done by hand, using knitting needles.

Why do you think knitting takes lots of practice?

You use two needles when you knit by hand.

All of these clothes are made out of wool.

Hat

Wool jacket

Tweed coat

Skirt

Wool can also be woven.

One of the most common fabrics made from woven wool is called **tweed.**

Are you wearing any wool clothing?

When we go outside, we wear shoes to protect our feet.

Do you know what your shoes are made out of?

Most leather comes from cows.

Most shoes are made out of **leather**. People make leather by soaking cows' skins in chemicals to make them softer and stronger.

18

The soles of shoes are often made out of **rubber**, which is a natural material made from **latex**.

Rubber bends easily and it is **waterproof**, so it's perfect for keeping your feet dry!

Latex flows from rubber trees into a bowl!

What else is waterproof to wear?

When it's raining outside, it's good to wear a waterproof coat, or carry an umbrella.

Waterproof fabric is often made out of **nylon**.

Do you know what nylon is?

Nylon is a **synthetic** fiber that is made from **oil**.

Oil is a **raw material** that formed under the Earth's surface millions of years ago from dead plants and animals.

This is an oil rig, which is a platform in the sea where the oil is drilled from the seabed.

Oil can also come from wells in the ground.

The oil is transported in a ship called an oil tanker.

It is taken to be processed in an **oil refinery.**

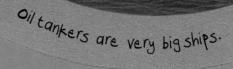

Oil tankers are very big ships.

This is an oil refinery.

Some of the oil is mixed with chemicals to make ribbons of nylon.

22

All of these clothes are made out of synthetic fibers...

The ribbons of nylon are melted and pushed through tiny holes, called **spinnerets**, to make thread.

The nylon thread is dried using jets of air, and wound onto reels, ready to be made into fabric.

Acrylic sweater

Polyester shorts

Nylon bathing suit

Nylon parka

Can you think of any other kinds of fabric?

23

Silkworms like to munch on leaves.

Silk fabric is soft and thin, but very strong.

Silkworms are the caterpillars of silk moths. They spin the silk fibers.

Silk is very expensive and is a luxurious fabric that not many people wear.

A field of hemp plants.

Hemp fabric is similar to cotton, but is a bit rougher. It comes from plants that are very easy to grow, so it is cheap to make.

It's much better for the environment than cotton because it uses less water and doesn't usually need any pesticides.

Silk is smooth and shiny.

This T-shirt is made from hemp fabric.

Bamboo fiber is thin and stretchy. It is a new kind of fabric made from bamboo, which is a type of grass.

Bamboo grows very quickly. Chemicals are used to turn the plant fibers into fabric.

This thermal vest is made from polar fleece.

Polar fleece is very soft and good at keeping you warm. It is made from a kind of plastic called polyethylene terephthalate (or PET for short), and it can even be made from recycled water bottles!

Bamboo plants growing.

Can you figure out which fabrics are natural, and which are synthetic?

Look them up in the glossary to find out the answers!

Wool

Cotton

Oil

The symbols on the map show the main parts of the world the raw materials for making different fabrics come from.

Which is closest to where you live?

Canada

Europe

Russia

United States

China

Africa

India

Pacific Ocean

South America

Australia

New Zealand

N
W E
S

Try to guess what your clothes are made out of.
Ask a friend to check the label for you. Were you right?

Take a look at the map, and see if you can find where it came from.

27

Glossary

Acrylic a synthetic fiber that feels like wool

Bamboo fiber a type of fabric made from natural fibers of bamboo plants

Boll a fluffy seedpod from the cotton plant

Button a small type of fastener, used by pushing it through a hole

Cotton a natural fiber made from the fluffy seed pods of cotton plants

Dyed when a cloth has been colored

Fabric cloth, textiles, or fabric are all woven or knitted materials

Fastener something used for holding fabric together

Fiber a long, thin part of a plant, animal, or mineral

Fleece the wool of a sheep before it has been processed

Hemp a fast-growing plant used to make natural fiber

Knitted fabric made by looping yarn or thread, using needles or a machine

Latex the sap of rubber trees, used to make rubber

Leather a natural material made from animal skin

Loom a machine used to make woven fabric

Natural existing in nature, not manmade

Nylon a synthetic fiber often used for waterproof clothes

Oil a greasy liquid also called petroleum

Oil refinery a factory where oil is purified

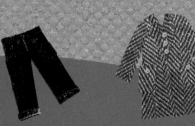

Organic grown without pesticides or other chemicals

Pesticides chemicals used by farmers to kill insects

Polar fleece soft fabric made from synthetic fibers

Polyester a synthetic fiber made from oil

Processed made using a series of different actions

Raw material a material before it has been processed

Rubber a natural material made from latex

Shearing cutting the fleece from a sheep to make wool

Sheep grazing animals that grow wool fleeces

Silk soft cloth made of natural fibers from silkworms

Silkworm caterpillar of the silk moth, which produces silk fibers

Spinneret part of a machine used to make synthetic fibers

Synthetic a man-made material, not found in nature

Thread thin type of string usually made from cotton or nylon

Tweed a type of cloth made from woven wool

Waterproof something that doesn't allow water to get in

Wool a natural fiber made from the fleece of a sheep

Woven fabric made by passing threads over and under each other using a loom

Yarn thread made from wool

Zipper a fastener with two rows of teeth

Index

This edition first published in 2013 by
Sea-to-Sea Publications
Distributed by Black Rabbit Books
P.O. Box 3263, Mankato, Minnesota 56002

Text and illustrations copyright
© Ruth Walton 2009, 2013

Printed in the United States of America,
North Mankato, MN

All rights reserved.

9 8 7 6 5 4 3 2

Published by arrangement with the
Watts Publishing Group Ltd., London.

Library of Congress Cataloging-in-Publication Data

Walton, Ruth.
  Let's get dressed / written & illustrated by Ruth
Walton. -- 1st ed.
     p. cm. -- (Let's find out)
  Includes index.
  Summary: "Discusses the different fibers and textiles
our clothing is made from, including cotton, wool,
and other natural and synthetic fabrics"--Provided
by publisher.
  ISBN 978-1-59771-383-2 (alk. paper)
  1. Clothing and dress--Juvenile literature. 2. Clothing
trade--Juvenile literature. I. Title.
TX340.W35 2013
391--dc23
                                                    2011052689

Series Editor: Sarah Peutrill
Art Director: Jonathan Hair
Photographs: Ruth Walton, unless
otherwise credited

Picture credits: I Stock Photo:
16b (Madeleine Openshaw), 17t (Susan Trigg),
18 (Gabriel Eckert), 19b (George Clerk), 22b
(Karen Merryweather), 24tl (Jason Gulledge),
24tr (ideeone), 25b (Kevin Russ). Shutterstock: 16t
(Gail Johnson). Every attempt has been made to
clear copyright. Should there be any inadvertent
omission please apply to the publisher for
rectification.

RD/6000006415/001
May 2012